Robot
Revolution

By Justin Reichman

www.av2books.com

Your AV² Media Enhanced book gives you an online audio book, and a self-assessment activity. Log on to www.av2books.com and enter the unique book code from this page to access these special features.

Go to www.av2books.com, and enter this book's unique code.

BOOK CODE

J137088

AV² by Weigl brings you media enhanced books that support active learning.

AV² Audio Chapter Book Navigation

HIGHLIGHTED TEXT   ACTIVITIES   HOME   CLOSE

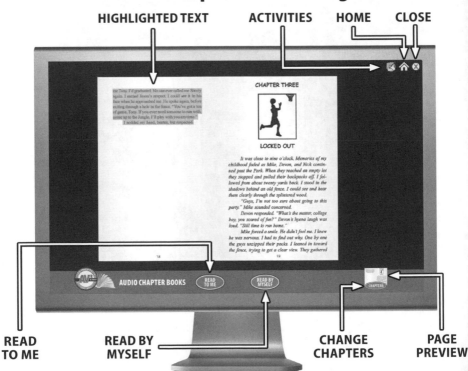

READ TO ME   READ BY MYSELF   CHANGE CHAPTERS   PAGE PREVIEW

Published by AV² by Weigl
350 5th Avenue, 59th Floor
New York, NY 10118

Website: www.av2books.com   www.weigl.com

Library of Congress Control Number: 2013937478
ISBN 978-1-62127-989-1 (hardcover)
ISBN 978-1-62127-945-7 (single-user eBook)
ISBN 978-1-48960-020-2 (multi-user eBook)

Printed in the United States of America in North Mankato, Minnesota
1 2 3 4 5 6 7 8 9 0   17 16 15 14 13

062013
WEP310513

First Published by Scobre Educational Press.

TABLE OF CONTENTS

CHAPTER ONE

ALONE IN THE UNIVERSE

Captain's Log: August 20, 1993
Day One Thousand Four Hundred.

I have not eaten or slept in almost four years. It is very cold and there is no oxygen to breathe. But I continue to press on. My last contact with a human was before the Berlin Wall fell in November 1989. I am totally alone in outer space. No one sends me any news. No one calls to say hello. I have absolutely nobody to talk to. I am so very bored.

Captain's Log: August 28, 1993
Day One Thousand Four Hundred Eight.

Finally, I had some excitement today. I took a close-up picture of a giant asteroid! The photo was the very first of its kind in the history of the world. Isn't that amazing? It's hard to photograph an asteroid because it moves so fast. (Some of them can travel up to 100,000 miles per hour.) Still, I managed to get one clean shot of it—wow!

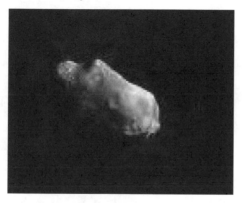

The lone photo taken of the asteroid, Ida.

After I took the photo, I sent it by satellite down to Earth. My picture showed that the asteroid was over 35 miles long. It's so big that it actually has its own tiny moon spinning around it. The scientists safe on Earth got to name my asteroid (even though I'm the one who put myself at risk to get the photo). They named it Ida. Personally, I would have named it Gigantor Supreme, but I won't complain. I never complain. I just do what I'm told.

Captain's Log: August 29, 1993
Day One Thousand Four Hundred Nine.

I'm still so bored. There is nothing to do. I don't have a book or even a deck of cards. There is no television. I still haven't eaten or slept, but I'm not hungry or tired. I continue to press on—all I do is press on.

My next stop is Jupiter. The scientists are sending me on a suicide mission. I will throw myself into Jupiter's atmosphere. Once there, I will be crushed into millions of tiny bits. That's because I'll experience forces of gravity over 350 times stronger than those of Earth.

Don't worry, I'm not scared. I will always do what I'm told. I will never get angry, frustrated, or worried. And I will never complain.

What kind of creature can live without air, food, sleep, and companionship for years on end? What sort of thing would follow every order, never asking a single question? Even when it is told to sacrifice itself?

Although the Captain's Log you just read is made up, the events in it really did happen. An explorer was launched into space on October 18, 1989. The explorer really did snap pictures of an asteroid over 35 miles long. It didn't eat, it didn't sleep, and it never complained. And believe it or not, it really did hurl itself into Jupiter's super-strong atmosphere. And then it exploded into millions of tiny bits.

This brave explorer was a robot, or more specifically, a space probe. It was nicknamed Galileo. The name originally belonged to the famous Italian math whiz, astronomer, and telescope innovator, Galileo Galilei.

This statue of Galileo stands in Florence, Italy.

Galileo (the robot) and other space probes have helped us learn more about the universe. These space probes, controlled by people on the ground, enter extremely dangerous environments. They take huge risks so that people don't have to.

After all, it's not that big a tragedy if a space probe crashes. Sure, tons of time, energy, and money go into creating these things. But unlike humans, robots are built to come and go. It's people you can't replace.

If you know anything about robots, you know they are pretty much the opposite of teenagers. Robots do whatever they are told. They don't complain. They don't talk back. They don't stay out past their curfew. They would never start a food fight.

Did you know that the word "robot" hasn't been around that long? "Robot" comes from the Czech word "robota," which means required or forced labor. The word robot was first introduced into the English language in 1923. That really wasn't *so* long ago.

As robots become more advanced, they become more useful to human beings. The space probe Galileo's job was perfect for a robot. Scientists shot this mechanical being out into space. They programmed it to complete tasks that they couldn't do themselves without risking their own lives. That's awesome when you think about it.

Robots are pretty new to the scene. Sure, they've been in Hollywood movies over the years. (Just a few of them are *Terminator*, *Star Wars*, *Robocop*, *A.I.*, *Transformers*, and *Short Circuit*.) But their existence in real life is a fairly new thing. In fact, robots have been building cars, flying around space, and doing other tasks for only a little over 50 years.

Robotics (the study of the design and use of robots) is on the cutting edge of technology. Scientists are imagining (and developing) a world where robots and human beings live side-by-side. In this world, robots work alongside people to make life better for everyone.

Imagine a world where a robot babysits your kid sister while you go to the mall!

The robotics movement *officially* started more than 50 years ago. In 1954, the first stationary (it stayed in one place) industrial robot was invented. The robot's name was Unimate, and he was pretty special. Unimate was basically a great big mechanical arm. He could be programmed to lift things up and down without anyone controlling him.

That may not sound very exciting now, but this *big* arm was a *big* deal in 1954. As photographs of Unimate began to circle the globe, people were amazed. They simply couldn't believe that the arm moved all by itself. The technology behind this mechanical arm was new, exciting, and profitable. In fact, in 1961, Unimate joined the assembly line at General Motors, helping to build cars!

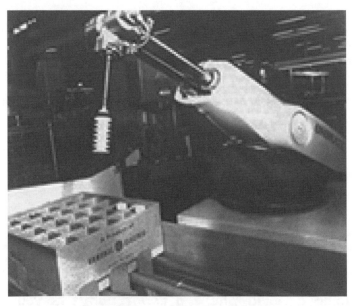

Unimate working in 1954.

Robot development exploded after the world found out about Unimate. Here was a worker that you didn't have to pay. He never took a break. And he would do the same thing over and over. He never slowed down, got bored, or needed to go to the bathroom. Suddenly, every business on the planet wanted to learn how robots could help them. These robots were being created by a new group of super-smart (and yes, sometimes super-nerdy) scientists.

As the technology advanced, the worldwide interest in robotics did, too. Thousands of talented men and women began pursuing robotics as a career. These brilliant and creative minds have developed some truly awesome robots.

Today, robots come in all shapes and sizes. They can be enormous and complex masses of metal. For example: the giant, car-smashing "Truckasaurus"—a humungous robot that smashes and "eats" automobiles in shows around the country.

> **Want to know more? Type in the word Truckasaurus at www.youtube.com and check out some really incredible footage!**

Robots can also be nearly invisible. Don't let their tiny size fool you, though. Sometimes the most incredible robots come in the smallest of packages. For example, a robot known as HeartLander is just 20 millimeters long. It looks sort of like a caterpillar. But this robot is way cooler than a caterpillar (and cater-pillars are pretty cool).

HeartLander is inserted onto the surface of a living person's heart! It travels across the heart to problem areas and delivers lifesaving drugs. That's right— a tiny machine that crawls on your heart while it is beating, and gives you medicine. Amazing!

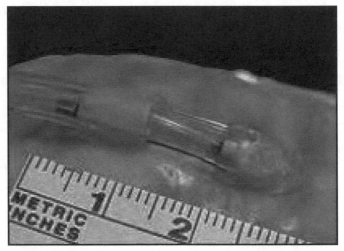

HeartLander is just a few inches long!

Nowadays, robots appear in places you wouldn't even think of. Robots make our cars. They clean our floors. They help us perform surgeries. They deliver our mail. Hordes of robots are working together to perform complex tasks, like landing on Mars. Robots are toys. Robots even star in movies. (Did you know that many newborn babies in films are actually robots?) Robots are our friends.

Yes, it's an exciting time for robots. And it's an exciting time to be creating them. It's only going to get a lot *more* exciting as the technology behind them advances. Some people say we'll soon have robots that can think and reason like humans do. Imagine that for a second—an "artificial intelligence" equal to our own.

That thought is amazing and scary at the same time. To be able to create something so complex is a very powerful thing. That technology needs to be in the right hands … like the hands of the young, brilliant subject of this book, Eletha Flores.

Of course, nobody is born with a passion for creating robots. Over time, and through life experiences, things just kind of happen. Your passions develop as you go along. Just ask Eletha.

CHAPTER TWO

LOOKING UP

"Wow, there's one!" 6-year-old Eletha said to her older brother, Lane. "There's another!" she shouted, as she nudged her younger brother, Pablo, and pointed straight up. "Did you guys see those?" Her big brown eyes reflected the lines of light streaking across the sky.

The three children were lying in the small patch of grass outside the Flores family's trailer. It wasn't much of a front yard. But it was a perfect spot to look up into the night sky. On this night, the sky was putting on a dazzling show. Three shooting stars soared overhead. A full moon shone brightly. To Eletha, staring up into the universe was better than staring at anything happening on Earth.

Eletha spoke excitedly to her brothers, "Do you realize that we are hanging upside down right now? We're sitting on a planet that is moving through space, and we're hanging from it! How amazing is that?"

"I'm going inside," said Lane, clearly unimpressed.

"Me, too," said Pablo.

"Fine," she sighed. "You guys just don't get it. I'll be out here—hanging."

Her brothers laughed and went inside. They knew their sister could stay outside and watch the stars all night. There was just something about outer space that drew her in. This is not to say that she wasn't interested in life on Earth—she definitely was. But the darkness above her head took up most of her thoughts.

On that same night, thousands of miles away, a blinking red light was moving through space. That light was attached to the robotic space probe, Galileo. It flashed 24 hours a day for more than four years.

Eletha was completely unaware of it at the time. But Galileo, and other space robots, would end up playing a big part in shaping her future.

During this time, Eletha, her two brothers, and her parents were living in Sulphur, Louisiana. Sulphur is a small town in the southern part of the state. It is located right next to a place called the Creole Nature Trail (Eletha's favorite place when she was 6).

The swampy Creole Nature Trail is called "Louisiana's Outback." It's home to alligators, snakes, hundreds of types of birds, and an amazing amount of shrimp. It's the kind of place where you don't want to get lost. If you do, you might end up being lunch for a hungry alligator.

The Trail is bursting at the seams with wildlife. When the birds migrate into the area, they come in full force. Thousands of these winged creatures turn the place into a living sea of feathers. The birds' songs, along with the insects' calls, combine to create unforgettable music.

When Eletha watched these birds, she wondered where they came from. *Where do these birds disappear to when winter comes? How high can they fly? Could they reach the stars?* She was thinking about how big the world outside Sulphur actually was. These thoughts also made her wonder what existed beyond the Earth.

At just 6 years old, Eletha was like a little sponge. She absorbed everything around her. Sometimes with her brothers, and sometimes alone, she would take long walks through the Creole Nature Trail. She often turned up rocks to see what was living under them. If she ever saw a snake, she didn't scream like most 6-year-olds would. In fact, she smiled.

Then she'd climb to the very tops of the trees and look out over the area. From that view, she was able to see "the big stuff all at once."

Like millions of other Americans, Eletha is of Mexican descent. Her father was born in Mexico, and her mother was born in Texas. Eletha has always been proud of her Mexican heritage.

Eletha felt that as a Mexican-American, she had an even bigger responsibility to be successful. That's because the opportunities for her in America were far greater than in her father's native country. She planned on taking advantage of these opportunities—even though she had no idea what they would be yet.

The Mexican flag.

Because of her Mexican heritage, Eletha realized that the United States was only one country of many on the globe. She often thought about Mexico, as well as countries like Sweden, Brazil, China, Poland, Australia, and Russia. She wanted to go to all these places and see what they were like.

Eletha also knew that Earth was only one planet among many in the universe. She started thinking about Mars and Saturn and Venus and Jupiter. *Did they have nature trails? What did the snakes look like under those rocks?* she wondered.

You probably already can see that Eletha was *a little different* from most other kids. She preferred reading books to watching television. She used big words and asked lots of questions that adults couldn't always answer.

Still, like most 6-year-olds, her favorite thing to do was play outside. In the summer, she spent hours designing and building "mud cities" in the hot Louisiana sun. (She was a natural builder, so her mud cities looked like real cities!)

To this day, Eletha can often be found reading a book.

She also really enjoyed figuring out how things work. When Eletha got a new toy, she liked to take it apart and put it back together. She did the same thing with stuff around the house. She's took apart things like the television remote, picture frames, and the door to her bedroom. And then she put them back together! Building things always came easily to her. She'd quickly turn a pile of Legos into complex structures.

Still playing with Legos. Above, is a working robot that Eletha designed and built ... using Legos!

Everything was going great for young Eletha. But behind the scenes, things were far from perfect. Her parents fought often, which scared Eletha. Being at home had become troubling and sad for her. Sometimes she just wanted to disappear.

The Flores family didn't have very much money. This made things extra hard on everyone. Some of her friends were able to afford nice clothes, dinners out at fancy restaurants, and family trips to the zoo. But Eletha's and her brothers' lives were a bit more limited.

Mr. and Mrs. Flores weren't always sure there would be enough money to pay for all the family's needs. Buying food and clothes was sometimes a real struggle. This was stressful for all of them. It also created a lot of tension inside their home—especially between Eletha's parents. Maybe that was part of the reason Eletha was so drawn to the outdoors.

One night, when her parents were having a fight, Eletha slammed the trailer door behind her and started to run. She ran and ran and ran, tears streaming down her face. *Why do they have to fight all the time?* she wondered. *Why can't they just stop?*

After a while, Eletha grew tired and lay down on the ground. As she caught her breath, she looked up at the sky. Far away from large cities, Sulphur's night sky was alive with countless sparkling stars. A bird flew overhead and Eletha sighed. "I wish I could fly," she whispered. "I wonder how far I would go."

During the next few hours, Eletha thought about her future. She decided right then and there to do something special with her life. *The universe is enormous, maybe endless*, she thought. *There must be something out there that was made just for me.*

Just as this thought made her smile slightly, she saw a shooting star. It had to be a sign. Eletha concentrated, and wished on that star. She wished that things would get better for her family at home. She wished that she could grow wings and fly along with the birds. More than anything, though, she wished that she would find her special place in the universe.

CHAPTER THREE

NOT ALL GOOD, AND NOT ALL BAD

In both life and science, sometimes things have to get worse before they get better. Take, for example, the events of December 6, 1957. The United States was trying to get a satellite into orbit. This was to compete with Russia (then known as the Soviet Union). A few months earlier, the Soviets had successfully launched a satellite into orbit for 96 days. It was called Sputnik. This was a really big deal at the time.

This competition between the United States and the Soviet Union was called the Space Race. Not wanting to come in second, the U.S. Navy spent tons of money and time building a satellite called Vanguard. (Vanguard is a lot less fun to say than Sputnik!)

Vanguard was ready for launch on December 6. Hundreds of reporters and television crews were there to film the event. Most Americans were listening in on their radios. Everyone wanted to see (or hear) Vanguard take off into space. This would prove that American skill and creativity were just as impressive as the Soviet Union's.

But Vanguard didn't even get off the ground. It toppled over and exploded on its launch pad in a fiery disaster. It was pretty embarrassing, to say the least.

The United States learned from the Vanguard disaster, though. Over 10 years later, the U.S. space program (now called NASA) did something incredible. The date was July 20, 1969. What happened? Well, the crew of the Apollo 11 spacecraft became the first group of people to step foot on the moon. Without a doubt, this moon landing moved the United States to the head of the Space Race.

The day Apollo 11 landed on the moon was a much better day for the United States than the day Vanguard blew up. It just goes to show that great success can be achieved through the process of trial-and-error.

The Flores family followed NASA's example and used trial-and-error in dealing with their ups and downs. When Eletha was 8 years old, her family moved from Sulphur, Louisiana, to Upper Marlboro, Maryland. They shared a house with another family. Eletha, her brothers, and her parents all lived on the first floor. The living quarters were tight, but this new house was definitely bigger than the trailer. So they were all pretty excited about their new digs.

For an 8-year-old, Eletha read a lot of books (at least two a week). She was very interested in learning. She was one of those rare kids who actually *wanted* to be at school. She didn't just read books for her schoolwork. At night, she would curl up in bed and read scary books just for fun. Her favorite thing to read was the *Goosebumps* series, but she also liked Stephen King's books.

In Upper Marlboro, Eletha could enjoy being outside, just like she did in Sulphur. Eletha, who already had developed a love of exploring, lost herself in the outdoors near her home. With her brothers, she raced through the fields surrounding her house. There was a forest nearby that seemed to go on forever. Eletha would explore deep into the woods, until the sticker bushes made it so she couldn't go any farther. Eletha loved being alone in the forest.

Eletha still hangs out in nature as often as she can...and now she brings friends with her, too!

Although all was going well outdoors, inside the Flores' home there was trouble. Her parents were fighting more and more. For Mr. and Mrs. Flores, the trial-and-error process was part of their marriage as well. For years, they had tried to make it work. But they just weren't making progress. They seemed to fight all the time.

The yelling was hard on Eletha and her brothers. Sometimes, Eletha would hide in her room. Usually, though, she would hide outside. Once again, she would find herself looking to the sky. Wherever Eletha hid, she could not make things better. She often wished that she could grow wings and fly away.

A few years later, Eletha's father moved out of the house, and her parents divorced. Divorce is never easy, and the Flores family struggled with it.

The day after the divorce was final, Eletha decided to run away from home. She packed up a few things in her backpack and snuck outside. Eletha ran and ran and ran as far as she could. She desperately wanted to get away from everything.

Just like the fish pictured above, running away seemed like a simple way to solve Eletha's problems.

About an hour later, she was deep in the woods and came upon a pond. It seemed like the perfect place for her to start over. Eletha stayed near the pond all day. "If I could hunt and fish, I would stay here and live happily forever," she said to no one in particular.

Pretty soon, she realized that living with the trees and talking to herself wouldn't solve her problems. She looked up at the sky again, and saw that the sun was close to setting. The wind started to pick up. She didn't have a coat with her, and she didn't know how to make a fire. Plus, there were no Slurpee machines in the woods! And Slurpees were Eletha's favorite snack. So she decided it was time to go home.

Eletha walked back through the dark woods alone. She felt scared and unsure about life without her father living in the house. Later that night, Eletha's mom found her alone in her room, crying.

Her mom sat down next to Eletha. "Why are you crying, little one?" she said.

"I don't know what we're going to do," sobbed Eletha. "I miss Dad. And I'm scared we won't be able to pay for everything."

"You know what, Eletha," said her mom, "I'm scared, too. But sometimes you have no choice. You just have to go through certain things. Your father and I weren't getting along, so we had to make a change. We're going to get through this together."

Eletha's mom was right. Over time, they *did* get through it together. Things were different after the divorce, though. Everyone had more responsibilities. The kids had to pitch in more around the house, because Eletha's mom was busy working all the time. The family joined together and became stronger.

The constant fighting had ended. Everyone started to notice something different around the house. It was quiet, peaceful, and happy. Sometimes, divorce can actually be the best thing for a family (even though it seems awful at the time).

The disastrous first Vanguard launch was tough for the United States to handle. Just like the initial split of the Flores family was difficult to deal with. But there was a silver lining in both cases. The divorce brought the family closer together. And the Vanguard failure pushed the U.S. space program to pull ahead in the Space Race.

Eletha realized she had been focusing too much on negativity, conflict, and the desire to escape. Now that all the yelling had stopped, she looked to the sky for help less often. She was able to focus a bit more on her life on Earth. After all, middle school was just around the corner. And this bright, curious 12-year-old was jumping into every opportunity she could find.

Left: Eletha jumps off Seneca Falls (not head first, but give her a break!) Right: Eletha flashes her million dollar smile.

CHAPTER FOUR

LOOKS CAN BE DECEIVING

Cockroach.

Just the word makes some people's stomachs churn. And it's no wonder. Cockroaches are slimy. They smell. Some of them hiss and make other nasty noises. Cockroaches gross out *a lot* of people.

Think about it. Could you climb into a bathtub filled with live cockroaches if someone dared you? Could you sit still and not scream while their shiny, hairy legs scurried all over your body? Could a cockroach burrow in your nose without making you scream?

Okay, I'll stop. My point is that cockroaches are pretty gross.

But are we being too hard on these insects? Are they more than just disgusting bugs? Can we actually *learn* something from them? There are a lot of people who think so.

Consider this: The cockroach is one of the oldest living winged insects. A cockroach today is pretty much the same cockroach that was around 320 million years ago! While the dinosaurs came and went, the cockroach remained. The insect has been on Earth over 2,000 times longer than humans. And they show no signs of going anywhere.

You won't even believe what's being done with cockroaches at the University of Tokyo. Scientists have put small robotic "backpacks" onto a number of their homegrown cockroaches. The tiny backpack is filled with electrodes. (Electrodes are basically devices that transmit electricity.) The scientists can "buzz" the electrodes with a remote control. Then, the cockroach will turn left or right, or more forward or backward. Their direction depends on where the scientist places the stimulation (or the buzz). In other words, the researchers have created a remote-controlled cockroach! I'm not making this up.

You're probably wondering why anyone would

spend time doing this kind of thing. Well, according to Assistant Professor Isao Shimoyama, head of the university's bio-robot team, "Insects can do many things that people can't."

For example, imagine the small spaces that a cockroach could get into. In an earthquake-damaged building, it could search for victims to rescue. Or, the "Robo-roach," as it's called, could be sent on spy missions. A true, living *bug*! These tiny robotic bugs could be sent into pretty much any room on the planet. And they would go completely undetected.

There are still some kinks to be worked out. Sometimes the cockroach doesn't go where the scientist directs it to go. And over time, the cockroach becomes less sensitive to the remote control. Still, you have to admit that the whole deal is pretty incredible. Someone has made a robot out of a living thing—*or made a living thing into a robot.*

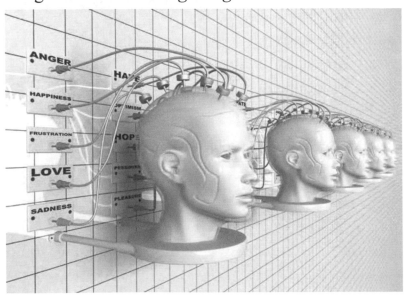

This brings up all kinds of questions. Is it possible to make a "living" robot in the future? What's the difference between an insect and a robot anyway? What does it mean to be alive? Will I ever be able to buy a team of cockroaches to take out the trash, do the dishes and clean my room? What about to challenge me in a game of *Halo 3*?

Who would have thought there was so much to learn from such a gross bug? Think of that the next time you judge something only from its outer appearance. People often say, "Don't judge a book by its cover." They could just as easily say, "Don't judge an insect by its nasty, hairy legs."

Like most of us, Eletha has been guilty of judging a book by its cover. In her case, it was Mr. Taylor. He was her seventh grade math teacher at James Madison Middle School. While by no means a cockroach, Mr. Taylor was not what you would call "cuddly."

On the first day of school, Eletha and her friend Marta walked quickly down the busy halls of James Madison.

Neither of them wanted to be late for class. Most of their hyper classmates were bumping around, yelling, shooting spitballs, laughing, and flirting. In other words, it was a typical first day of school.

As you know by now, Eletha is not *typical* at all. She was totally, 100% ahhhhhh-anxious on her first day of school! You see, middle school was not the best time for Eletha. The kids who do the best in school don't always do the best in popularity contests. Eletha got nearly perfect grades, but she often felt awkward around her fellow students. How many friends did she have? Well, she could count them on one hand. Without using all of her fingers!

Eletha had plenty of "alone time" during her middle school years.

A lot of kids at school seemed to be content lounging in the halls and goofing off. Eletha, on the other hand, was focused on spending her time learning. She was often frustrated, though. She felt that her teachers were too busy dealing with the kids who were misbehaving. As a result, the classes they taught weren't as challenging as they could be. (In the defense of the teachers at James Madison: It's hard to challenge someone who happens to be among the smartest young people on the planet!)

"What's your next class?" Marta asked Eletha.

"I've got Mr. Taylor for math," said Eletha.

Marta stopped dead in her tracks. "Whoa. I heard that guy is crazy."

"What do you mean?" asked Eletha. "It's algebra. It's supposed to be good."

"Only you would think that algebra is supposed to be good. Haven't you heard about Mr. Taylor? He's a total psycho. Last year, he ate a kid's cat because he was mad at him for turning in his homework late."

"Oh, come on," said Eletha. "Do you really believe that?"

"Well, I've heard lots of other things about Mr. Taylor, too," said Marta. "Bottom line, he's nuttier than a fruitcake."

No, this isn't Mr. Taylor, but you get the point, right?

Hearing Marta's words disappointed Eletha. She sighed dramatically. *Algebra is the one class that I was excited about this year*, she thought. *It figures that it's being taught by some lunatic. Perfect.*

By this point, Eletha had reached Mr. Taylor's door. "Good luck," said Marta as Eletha disappeared into a sea of hyper kids.

When class began two minutes later, it appeared that Marta was right about Mr. Taylor. He was an unusual, scary, gruff-looking man. He was wearing a leather vest, and his hairy forearms were covered with tattoos. He stood in front of the class with his arms folded. "OK, take your seats," he grumbled. "And do it quickly."

Who is this terrifying man? Eletha thought.

Instantly, everyone in class did as they were told. Mr. Taylor was the kind of guy you listened to. It wasn't just the way he looked—it was the way he talked, too. It's easy to judge a cockroach as being a gross bug. And it was just as easy to judge Mr. Taylor as being a scary and strange man.

A few months earlier, Eletha had aced a math placement test. This landed her in Mr. Taylor's advanced algebra class. She *had been* excited about this class. She actually felt like it was going to teach her something new about mathematics. But she was now convinced that she was in for another boring class (taught by a psychopath, no less).

Just as Eletha was about to give up all hope, something happened. Mr. Taylor began teaching. And guess what? He turned out to be a math-teaching machine. He actually got the kids excited about math. Eletha had never before met anyone like Mr. Taylor.

By the end of that first semester, Eletha was starting to connect everything to math. Her entire understanding of the world (and the universe) seemed to be one big math equation. *Everything is math,* she reasoned. *And math is everything.*

$$R_s \cdot T \cdot \int_{V_1}^{V_2} \frac{1}{V} \, dv = m \cdot R_s \cdot T \, | \, ln$$
$$\cdot R_s \cdot ln(V_2) - m \cdot R_s \cdot ln(V_1) = $$
$$(V_2) - (ln(V_1)) = m \cdot R_s \cdot T \cdot ln$$
$$= m \cdot R_s \cdot ln\left(\frac{V_2}{V_1}\right), \quad W = -m \cdot$$

Mr. Taylor's class made Eletha more excited than she had ever been about any subject. She would get butterflies in her stomach as she walked into math class. Yes, Mr. Taylor demanded a lot from his students. But for the most part, they didn't mind. In fact, they respected him for it. Learning how math connected to real life was something most of them had never thought about. It was awesome.

The class was also entertaining beyond math. You see, Mr. Taylor was a pretty funny man. He had a strong love of the singer Bruce Springsteen, also known as "The Boss." His love of The Boss bordered on obsession.

Mr. Taylor had a way of helping his students

make certain connections. For example, he showed them that math is the "building block" from which the field of computer science was born. If there were no math, there would be no computer science. And if there were no computer science, there would be no robots. "Learning math," he explained, "is the key to unlocking the secrets of the universe."

That's because math is the language of technology. Numbers (and the way they relate to each other) are at the core of every great technological invention. For example, do you know how the Internet works? Through numbers and math—that's how!

Pictured to the right, is binary code, which is the mathematical language spoken by computers.

When you type in a website address, your computer is sent a complex signal. That signal is based on numbers and code. It tells the computer how to build the webpage you requested—from colors to text to images—in an instant.

A new world had been opened up to Eletha. It was a world that started with math. And it ended as far away as the stars, which is where Eletha was headed next. Well, almost.

CHAPTER FIVE

YOUR AVERAGE TEENAGE ROCKET SCIENTIST

Eletha knew she loved math, so what was her next step? Getting involved with NASA, of course. (You have to dream big, right?) Eletha knew she wanted to learn more about science, and what better place to learn than NASA?

Science helps us to understand what things are made of and how they work. It puts the power to improve the world in people's hands. Eletha says, "Science is the uncovering of nature's secrets. It lets us use the resources we already have in new and innovative ways."

Mr. Taylor's math class from three years earlier had fueled Eletha's interest in science and robotics. And she took off like a rocket from there. She began reading every book she could find on topics that really interested her. She read books about things like robotics, the study of the universe, engineering, and quantum physics (not exactly "light reading"). The next step was to find a way into NASA.

Above, is the rocket garden at NASA's Kennedy Space Center in Florida. Below, is a photo of the cockpit of a NASA space shuttle.

The Goddard Space Flight Center, which is part of NASA, was pretty close to where Eletha lived. She often visited their website to see if they had any programs she could get involved with. Indeed they did. But there was no real application process. So Eletha asked around until she found something that was available and interesting to her. That's how Eletha ended up spending a summer that would change her life.

After her sophomore year, Eletha took part in a program with NASA engineers at Goddard. While a lot of girls her age were hanging out at the mall, Eletha was using her time a little differently. She was hanging out with a bunch of geniuses at NASA!

They are doing some pretty hefty research at Goddard. But Eletha wasn't intimidated at all. Instead, she was excited. "I was interested in learning about careers in research and development. I needed to see if I wanted to work in science and engineering for life," explains Eletha.

So how would a 16-year-old try to figure that out? Well, Eletha sat in on research team meetings. She listened to how high-tech projects are developed and managed. She took notes and paid attention to the details. She heard from engineers, scientists, and managers from all backgrounds … while they worked together on a real project!

Typical sophomore summer vacation, huh?

Eletha observed one project in particular. It was headed by a group of scientists who were building micro-electro-mechanical shutters for space tele-scopes. Micro-electro-mechanical what? Eletha, please explain. "The shutters were designed to allow specific types of light to enter the telescope. The point was to target certain sources of light while blocking out others," says Eletha.

In very basic terms, Eletha was working with scientists who were creating a special kind of tele-scope. The shutters on the telescopes allowed for deeper exploration into space. And this lets scientists learn more about the universe without leaving Earth. That is pretty darn exciting.

Keep in mind that Eletha sat in rooms with people at least twice her age. They had fancy PhDs and years of experience in the field—and she was hang-ing with them just fine. In fact, she was blooming. She loved spending time working at Goddard. After all, this was a place where it was cool to be smart and excited about science and learning.

That summer helped Eletha's future come into focus. She decided that she was definitely interested in being some type of scientist. And a group of ro-bots was about to help her figure out exactly where he wanted to go next.

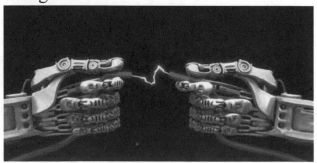

CHAPTER SIX

GET IT TOGETHER

When people work on something as a group, the result is sometimes better than if all those people had been working by themselves. Think about this example: Imagine a violinist playing the violin. The violinist has been practicing, so she is really good. Can you hear (in your head) the notes of someone rocking out on a violin? It's pretty beautiful, right? Now imagine a whole room of talented musicians playing music together. Can you hear that? A symphony is simply amazing—often even more amazing than when a musician plays alone. This concept is called "synergy." People have created a lot of cool things through synergy.

Have you ever thought about what it would be like if a bunch of *robots* worked together? Is that even possible? You bet it is.

Eletha designed and built the above robot.

In fact, scientists are doing lots of amazing research with groups of robots. A group of robots working together is called a swarm. It's a slightly terrifying term (as in a "swarm of killer bees"). But in this case, a swarm simply refers to a bunch of robots working together on a common task. That task is usually something like exploring space. (Not, say, stinging people in the head and taking over the planet.)

A swarm of robots can contain as few as 10 robots, or as many as 10,000! You may have heard of the Roomba, a robot designed by a company called iRobot. Basically, the Roomba is a robot vacuum. It cleans your floor while you get to put your feet up and eat ice cream.

The brilliant scientists at iRobot are also working on something they call the SwarmBot. The SwarmBot is a little guy—just a 5-inch cube, actually.

But crammed into that tiny body are some complex mechanics and software. These allow the SwarmBot to move around quickly, sense other objects, and communicate with other SwarmBots.

Right now, SwarmBots can perform several tasks. They can gather together at a certain point of interest. They can navigate long distances. And they can explore the layout of a building, and even create a map. How cool is that? SwarmBots are released into a building, where they split up. Then they each explore a different space. Working together, they create a map of that entire building. (Keep in mind that none of them explored more than one small piece of the building on their own.)

This may not sound like a whole lot. But remember, SwarmBots are performing these tasks without a single human controlling them! That is the genius of SwarmBots. It takes a lot of time and effort to control something millions of miles away. And the control doesn't always work. Imagine sending a team of robots that can control themselves into space to check out the environment. This type of thing is the next generation of space exploration.

There are no known living beings on Mars or other planets. That fact makes these kinds of robotic developments very important. Plus, isn't it pretty amazing to think of a bunch of machines working together in space? It's almost like we're sending something alive out into the universe.

SwarmBots can also be used for search and rescue missions. Think back to the remote-controlled cockroach. Imagine a group of tiny robotic creatures exploring something like a collapsed building. All the while, they'd be able to communicate with each other. They would probably be able to rescue a lot more people than a bunch of robots working alone.

The cockroach isn't the only insect that robot-scientists are studying. They are taking a close look at *all* the social insects. Social insects are called "social" because they live in groups, have specialized roles, and can communicate with one another. (Not because they sign each other's yearbooks, and make out under the bleachers at football games.) Examples of social insects include bees, termites, and ants—all insects that work together.

Which way's the party, dude?

By the time her senior year rolled around, Eletha became a lot more social herself. "As I took control of my academic life, I stopped worrying about what other people thought," says Eletha. "This helped me loosen up a bit and have some more fun. Once you're comfortable in your own skin, things have a way of falling into place."

Eletha became a much happier teenager. She decided that, while her academic career was important, the people in her life were important, too. She'd learned a critical lesson: "No matter how pumped you are about school and your future, you can't ignore the people around you."

Eletha and friends.

That didn't mean that Eletha had stopped pursuing her dreams. No chance of that. In fact, around this same time, Eletha took an important internship that changed her life. It was with Goddard's **A**utonomous **N**ano**T**echnology **S**warm team (simply known as ANTS).

Once again, Eletha found out about this program on her own. She made an appointment to meet with the people in charge of the ANTS team. She talked with them about getting an internship with the group. (Nanotechnology refers to a branch of science that looks at things on the molecular and atomic levels.)

Soon after, Eletha got involved with an exciting swarm project. "I helped build models of a tetrahedral robotic arm. And I assembled printed circuit boards for operating a 700-pound 12-tetrahedral robotic walker," says Eletha, matter-of-factly. "Basically, it's a giant robot that can move around in cool ways."

Huh?

To explain a little more, the 12-tetrahedral robotic walker looks like a walking jungle gym. It can change its shape to practically anything. The robot's shape-changing ability allows it to walk over the unknown surfaces of other planets. And that is totally amazing.

> **Want to learn more? To see the robotic walker in action, check out the ANTS homepage at: http://ants.gsfc.nasa.gov.)**

These types of swarming robots are the future of space exploration. The robots will be able to explore on their own. They won't need any help or contact from humans. They will communicate with each other and pass along loads of information, videos, and photos back to Earth. And if one of them blows up (or is eaten by a giant space monster!), it's not that huge of a deal. Another one can always be built—unlike its human creators.

Eletha was on the fast track to becoming one of those robot creators. She was developing a strong love of robotics: "The field of robotics is like the highest point of all engineering awesomeness. The power that humans have with robots is incredible. Especially in relation to outer space."

A lot of different fields of study come together in robotics. Eletha excitedly explains, "Everyone gets a chance to play—computer scientists, mechanical engineers, electrical engineers, and craftsmen." A single robot is the result of combining knowledge from all these fields. Talk about synergy at work.

"I like robotics because I can make a robot do whatever I program it to," says Eletha. "I like that power. By designing a robot's brain, I can make it perform tasks just for me." When a working robot is created, it truly is like creating a real, living thing.

With such a passion for robotics, what was next for this budding scientist? Well, she had to graduate high school first. ...

High school graduation is an exciting time. For the first time in your life, *you* get to decide what happens next. Do you go to college? Do you go to work? Do you go live in the woods? What path are you going to follow? The choice is yours.

Graduation is also a strange time. Part of you is still a kid, and another part is moving toward adulthood. Eletha recalls this bittersweet experience, and the family drama that followed: "I was delivering the valedictorian address. So I got to walk on stage and give a speech in front of thousands of people. I love public speaking, even though it was kind of scary.

Eletha's valedictorian speech wasn't her last adventure in public speaking. Above, Eletha makes her speech after being honored as a winner of the prestigious Hispanic Heritage Youth Award for Engineering and Mathematics.

"At the end, people said they loved my speech, which made me really happy. While it was happening, I was focused on not getting too emotional—absolutely no tears allowed! So I kept telling myself that it's really no big deal. It's just graduation.I had to keep the nerves down. Once my speech was over, I kinda felt like it really *wasn't* that big of a deal.

"After the ceremony, I tried to find my parents. My mother was there with her fiancé, Tom. My father was there with both my brothers, too. My dad doesn't like the fact that my mom is remarrying. He gives Tom a really hard time. Dad kind of made the whole thing into an awkward, uncomfortable, look-at-your-shoes moment.

"Anyway, the most awkward moment came next. Mom and Tom were standing to my right. Dad and my little brother were to my left, and my older brother was next to me. My dad turns to me and asks if I want to go out to eat with him as a celebration.

"The inner turmoil I felt at that moment is how I feel every time there is a Mom-Dad confrontation. I was literally made to choose between my parents—again. If I were to go with my dad, I would have to leave my mother and brothers. I'd have to sit in the backseat of his truck, on top of random junk and tools. And I was wearing my brand-new, beautiful, white, satiny graduation dress and satin shoes. But saying no would mean going against Dad and being on Mom's side. That was terrible, too.

"Luckily, I had an appointment with my counselor that day. So I couldn't go out to eat with anyone right then. I was so glad I had an excuse not to have to make that decision at that moment.

"Despite the family stuff, I have good memories of that day. What I remember most clearly is that I gave the valedictorian speech, and the crowd cheered loudly. And my white dress … and my mom smiling and my brother Lane smiling and giving me a hug. And my friends smiling, and how we were all happy and planning parties. Good times."

CHAPTER SEVEN

A PLACE FOR ROBOTS AND THE PEOPLE WHO LOVE THEM

Hub of the Solar System. Hub of the Universe. American Athens. Beantown. City of Baked Beans. City of Kind Hearts. Whatever you want to call it, Boston, Massachusetts, is a historic city with an impressive past. People who love Boston *really* love Boston. And there's a lot to love.

Boston has a rich history. The city was a major player in the American Revolutionary War. Do you remember learning about the Battle of Lexington and Concord? Well, it happened outside of Boston. Also, guess where the Boston Tea Party and the Boston Massacre happened? That's right—Boston. Boston was also where Paul Revere took his famous ride.

The city is home to many "firsts." Boston was the first U.S. city to build a subway, and the first city in the country to get a park. It was also the U.S. city with the first medical school specifically for women.

In 2006, Boston was the first place where people lit 29,000 jack-o'-lanterns at the same time, setting a new world record. Any way you slice it, as far as cities go, Boston is impressive. (Speaking of slices, Boston Cream Pie is the official dessert of the entire state of Massachusetts.)

Boston is also home to some *serious* brainpower. Two of the most prestigious learning institutes in the world are in the Boston area. One is Harvard. The other is MIT, which stands for Massachusetts Institute of Technology.

MIT is one of the most impressive research institutes on the planet. A whopping 63 current or former members of the MIT community have won the Nobel Prize. (That's pretty much the biggest award you can hope to win in science.) Within the walls of MIT, there have been a ton of amazing inventions and innovations.

> **Want to learn more? Here is just a tiny sampling of the recent robot-related highlights from MIT's website, www.web.mit.edu:**

1994: MIT engineers develop a robot that can "learn" exercises from a physical thera pist, guide a patient through them, and—for the first time—record data on the patient's condition and progress.

1999: MIT engineers invent the first microchip that can store and release chemicals on demand. Potential applications   include jewelry that emit different scents depending on your mood, and "pharmacies" that could be swallowed or im-planted under the skin and programmed for the delivery medicine at specific times.

2002: MIT researchers create the world's first acrobatic   robotic bird—a small helicopter that the military could use in mountainous and urban combat.

As you would expect, some pretty "heavy hitters" hang out on the MIT campus. Its robotics department is considered to be one of the best in the world. And perhaps in the galaxy.

Consider Cog. Cog is part of MIT's Artificial Intelligence Laboratory. Cog is a robot that looks sort of like a human from the torso up. Cog has cameras for eyes and microphones for ears. There are a bunch of gyroscopes (spinning wheels) and motors in its head and arms. Cog will look at you. Cog's eyes will follow you around the room. Cog will play with a *Slinky*.

Interactions with Cog make you question whether you're looking at a bunch of parts, or a living thing. By studying Cog, the researchers aren't just learning about artificial intelligence. They are also learning about what it means to be a human being. Cog, pictured below, is part of MIT's Artificial Intelligence Labaratory. It's pretty amazing to see it in action.

Want to learn more? Check out Cog and it's creators at: www.ai.mit.edu/ projects/hu- manoid-robot- ics-group/cog.

There is a ton of other amazing stuff going on here. They're making robots that can talk. And they're building more and more advanced artificial limbs (arms and legs). Artificial limbs are made from a combination of mechanical and electrical parts. People who have lost one or more limbs can use them. They are able to move like real arms and legs.

They're also making robots that are learning how to recognize human emotion. There are crazy robotic swarms going on. There are robots that can fly. There are robots that can swim. There are teeny-tiny microscopic robots being built.

 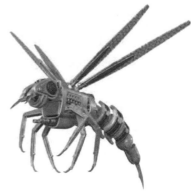

MIT is *the* place to be for robots, computer science, and artificial intelligence. As soon as Eletha learned about MIT, she was sure it was the place for her.

"I knew that MIT was the number one engineering school in the country. Going to school there was my highest, most far-reaching goal at that point," says Eletha. "It seemed like the ultimate challenge and opportunity to learn engineering. And engineering gives you the power to solve problems, create and design things, and change the world."

There was just one thing standing in the way of Eletha achieving her goal of getting into MIT. First, she had to get past MIT's very tough admissions process. Every year, about 12,000 of the smartest math and science students apply to get into MIT. And every year, about 10,500 of them end up very disappointed.

So what is the admissions process? First you apply, and then your application is reviewed by a senior MIT staff member. If your application is viewed as being competitive, it is passed on to a selection committee. Next, the selection committee weighs in. If the committee gives a good review, your application is sent to the Dean of Admissions. The Dean of Admissions will then personally look over your application. When all is said and done, about 12 people will spend a ton of time discussing your application. And deciding if you will get into MIT.

For Eletha, the process was extremely stressful. She submitted her application in the fall after spending lots of time on it. Then she waited and waited, and waited some more. All the while, she wondered, *What will these 12 people think of my application?*

CHAPTER EIGHT

IT'S IN THE MAIL

Some days, getting the mail is more life-changing than others. For instance, imagine if you won a contest and the mail carrier was delivering a giant check for $10 million. Well, that would be a pretty important mail day.

For mail carriers, though, most days of delivering the mail are exactly the same. This is especially true for one mail carrier. He is rather large, weighing in at 590 pounds. Every day, he performs his route without resting or eating. He doesn't stop to chat, and he is not afraid of dogs.

As you have probably guessed, we're talking about a robot. His name is Mailmobile, and he's an automated, robotic mail carrier. Mailmobile looks like a giant cart, with lots of little shelves for different people's mail. There's even a locking box for private stuff. Mailmobile travels around offices and goes up and down elevators. And this mail carrier can carry up to 800 pounds of mail.

You can program Mailmobile to do a number of tasks. He can open doors, and make a noise when he's rounding a corner, so as not to run someone over. Mailmobile will never complain about doing the exact same thing every day. Best of all, Mailmobile does all of this without ever wearing shorts, knee-high socks, or a funny hat!

Eletha, of course, is not a robot. So on some days, getting the mail is more exciting than others. There was one day she will never forget. That day, she discovered an envelope with a return address that read: MASSACHUSETTS INSTITUTE OF TECH-NOLOGY.

Eletha didn't know what to do. She wanted to open the envelope, but what if she didn't get in? And what if she *did* get in? Where would she be spending the next four years of her life? The answer was in the envelope.

With trembling hands, she took a deep breath and opened the letter. And then …

"I stared at the admissions papers in awe, mostly

silently," Eletha recalls. "Then I screamed and ran around the house shouting, 'I got in!'"

As soon as Eletha's mom heard the news, she started crying. Pablo and Lane were proud of their sister, too. When she called her father, he was thrilled as well.

Opening that envelope was like opening a giant party. Everyone was excited for Eletha. Mr. Taylor couldn't be happier. Her friends at school started calling her by the nickname "MIT."

So, one major goal was met. Eletha had been accepted at MIT. But things were really just getting started. There is a whole new world out there for her to discover. A world that is challenging, scary, fun, and unknown, all at the same time.

Eletha always seems to be searching for something. Above, she is exploring a cave.

In 2008, Eletha began the spring semester of her sophomore year at MIT. She is mostly adjusted, and she loves her new roommate.

Always the go-getter, Eletha has declared a double major (which means that she basically has *two* majors). One is in electrical engineering and the other is in computer science.

Since she arrived at MIT, Eletha has learned a lot both inside and outside the classroom. Her professors are amazing. "They love what they do, and some of them are really funny. All of them are smart, interesting to get to know, and have really great stories to tell," she explains.

Eletha is making new friends, too. She thinks the students are one of the best parts of MIT. "They are inspiring. They are caring and open, and they have neat backgrounds—some are international, with cool accents. They are fun to be around and are smart and capable, if a little crazy at times. And they are helpful with doing problem sets."

When she's not studying, Eletha loves to explore the outdoors, just like when she was little. She also loves Boston. One of the best things about living at MIT is that she can take the subway all over. She can go downtown, to Fenway Park where the Red Sox play, or even to Harvard Square.

The city and people are indeed great. But the best part is that at school, Eletha is actually creating robots! She is learning firsthand what it takes to make a functioning robot. And she is finding out just how challenging it is.

Making a robot is a process that takes a lot of time and thought. There are lots of steps involved. The first thing you have to do is figure out the purpose of the robot. What task is it going to be designed for? What do you want your robot to do? You have to answer these questions before you start anything.

Then, you have to figure out what you're going to make the robot out of. Next, you sketch what your robot is going to look like. Some people sketch on paper, while others use a computer. You can also give your robot a name at this stage.

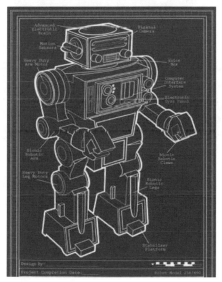

The next step may be the most difficult: You've got to work out the computer programs to make the robot behave the way you want it to. This part is like making the "brain" of the robot. You have to program the robot's microprocessor (its brain) to do what you want it to do.

Now, you've got to start building this thing. That means attaching the computer parts to wires, motors, and sensors—so that the microprocessor can actually tell the motors and sensors what to do. This process involves using something called a soldering iron. It's a device that looks a little bit like a screwdriver. The soldering iron is a little different, though. It gets really hot so you can melt solder (which is a melty metal). With it, you can join things like wires together.

And we're not even close to being done yet.

After it's built, you have to test your robot. Is it doing what you want it to? Is it doing the complete opposite of what you want it to do? Is it catching on fire? This step is the most frustrating. That's because most of the time, there are unexpected flaws that crop up during testing. Then you have to take the thing apart and fix it. Many times this leads to starting completely over.

Taking this robot apart was easy. Figuring out why it didn't work, and then putting it back together... not so easy.

While Eletha loves creating robots in school, the process can be quite overwhelming. "This robotics class I'm part of is kicking my butt," Eletha explains. "I've been really busy. I'm working on a robot right now, and I'll probably be here all night."

Eletha is surrounded by some of the brightest minds in the country. People expect a lot from her, and the pressure can be a little much at times. But most things that are worth doing are not easy, and Eletha is ready to give it her all.

Even at her young age, Eletha is already giving back. During the summer of 2008, she was an instructor at an MIT program for middle school students. Eletha plans to continue providing excitement and encouragement to kids. One day, perhaps she will be like a Mr. Taylor to a curious mind. (Although she will not make anyone sing Bruce Springsteen, unless they really want to.)

Does Eletha think of herself a role model? Yes. "I would definitely consider myself a role model for young Latinas. I have stood by my beliefs of doing well in school. And I have pursued electrical engineering and computer science—fields where you don't usually see as many Latinas," Eletha explains.

"I want to show young girls everywhere—Latinas in particular—that they can also achieve success. I want them to see that they have no reason to give up or shy away from dreaming big. Because if I can do it, they can, too."

All the winners of the Hispanic Heritage Youth Awards for Engineering and Mathematics.

Who knows what kinds of robots are going to be around in the future? We can guess, but no one can be certain. That's what's pretty cool about it. The same goes for Eletha. What's next for her? She's got some ideas, but she can't be 100% sure about any of them.

And what's next for you? If you think you might be interested in a career in science, Eletha has some advice for you. "I would encourage you to dive into your education. Become excited about learning new things and dreaming up changes you want to make in the field. Seek summer programs or high schools that offer science, math, engineering, and technology education. Apply for an internship or volunteer position on a research team at a local university to gain hands-on experience."

Sometimes, reaching your goals is difficult. You may falter. You may fail. But, only you can decide to give up or to keep going. Consider the following robot story:

In 1986, Honda, the car company, decided to make a robot. Not just any robot. One that could walk on two legs like a human. They had no idea how challenging this would actually be. But they did not give up.

After over a decade of research, failures, frustrations, and small and big successes, they did it. They finally had made a robot that could walk on its own! They named the robot Asimo.

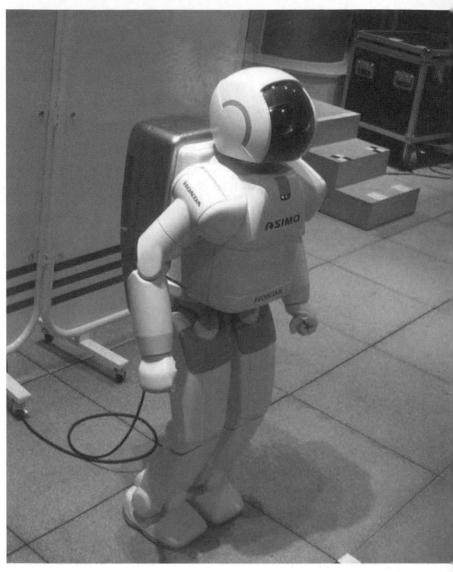

The original Asimo ... Honda's amazing, walking robot.

But why stop there? If they made a walking robot, what else could they do? Well, they rolled up their sleeves for another nine years and made a robot that could run. That's a total of 19 years of development—longer than the time Eletha has been alive. It just goes to show you that most things worth doing take a lot of effort.

The story of Asimo the robot is an important one to remember. It shows that before you can run, you have to learn to walk. And that can take some time. If you're thinking of a career in robotics, consider all the small steps you can take to make it happen. These small steps have a way of adding up to big steps. And pretty soon, you might find yourself developing a team of robotic space explorers.

So go start walking … so you can begin running!